START·A·CRAFT

Decorative Painting

Get started in a new craft with easy-to-follow
projects for beginners

SALLY RICHMOND

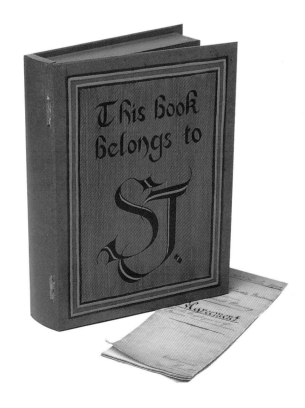

CHARTWELL
BOOKS, INC.

A QUINTET BOOK

Published by Chartwell Books
A Division of Book Sales, Inc.
PO Box 7100
Edison, New Jersey 08818-7100

This edition produced for sale
in the U.S.A., its territories
and dependencies only.

ISBN 0-7858-0320-3

This book was designed and produced by
Quintet Publishing Limited
6 Blundell Street
London N7 9BH

Creative Director: Richard Dewing
Designer: James Lawrence
Project Editor: Diana Steedman
Editor: Lydia Darbyshire
Photographer: Paul Forrester

Typeset in Great Britain by
Central Southern Typesetters, Eastbourne
Manufactured in Singapore by Eray Scan Pte Ltd
Printed in China by Leefung-Asco Printers Ltd

DEDICATION

**To my Mother, for being a constant source
of encouragement and support.**

Many thanks to the following for their help in
supplying items for the projects:
Paul Richmond, Helen Richmond,
Belinda Ballantine, Ann Witchell
and to Daler-Rowney, suppliers of
Fine Arts and Graphic materials

CONTENTS

INTRODUCTION

A close colleague and I have a favorite saying: "If it will stand still for long enough, paint it."

Paint is an exciting medium with endless potential, and it can be used to transform rather plain, rather unexciting or battered items into unusual, pretty things. If you are already interested in painting, you are likely to have come across different kinds of articles that you would like to decorate, but you may not be quite sure how to begin.

There are several different types of paint that can be used, and different paints are suitable for different surfaces. However, once you know what paint is appropriate, you will be able to experiment and transform practically every room in your home. Secondhand junk can become family heirlooms, and familiar, everyday items will become unrecognizable.

Remember, though, that an object that is inherently unattractive will always be unattractive, no matter what you do to the surface. Do not waste time trying to transform an object that you will never want to have in a room with you. On the other hand, pieces of furniture and ornaments that are just a bit tattered or worn or rusty, but that are elegant or pleasingly proportioned are well worth rejuvenating.

This book explains how to prepare a variety of surfaces so that they will accept decorative paint, and it will show, by working through a variety of articles, how different techniques and finishes can be applied.

MATERIALS AND TECHNIQUES

PAINTS

Artists' acrylic paints, which come in tubes, are available in a huge variety of colors from most stores supplying artists' materials. All the colors can be intermixed, and because acrylics are water-based, they can be dissolved in, and mixed with, water. When they are dry, they are waterproof and can only be removed with denatured alcohol. They are fast-drying and are, therefore, ideal for design work because there is little danger that you will smudge them. Acrylic paints can be used on water- or alcohol-based paints, and they can sometimes be made to adhere on top of oil-based paints if you add a tiny amount of liquid detergent to them. Clean your brushes in water.

Artists' oil paints, which are also available in tubes and can be found in art stores, look much like acrylic paints. They contain linseed oil, however, and are, therefore, classified as oil-based. Like other oil-based products, they can be dissolved with turpentine or mineral spirits, which should be used to remove the paint when it has dried and to clean your brushes. They can be used on almost any surface.

Water-based acrylic varnish

Latex

Enamels

Ceramic paint

Shellac

Casein paint

Metal paint

Artists' acrylic and oil paints

Latex paint is water-based, and it is probably most often associated with home decorating. All hardware stores and those selling home decorating materials will stock latex paints, and many of the larger stores have color-mixing machines, which are invaluable because so many of the standard paints come in pastel shades. You may find it useful to buy a small range of dark colors and white and to mix your own colors. Look for small, trial-size cans, which are ideal for furniture and small items and which are often made in unusual colors.

Latex paint needs a porous surface to adhere to, although it will also cover alcohol-based paints and varnishes. Clean your brushes in water. When latex paint is dry, it is waterproof and can then be removed only with denatured alcohol.

Acrylic primer/undercoat, which is also water-based, is widely available in hardware and home decorating stores. It is similar to latex paint, but has an acrylic binder, which makes it stronger. Use it to

seal and prime bare wood. It is only available in white, so you will need to use shellac as a primer if you are planning to use a dark top coat. Clean your brushes in water.

Casein or buttermilk paint, which is made from a by-product of cheese-making, is another water-based paint, but it remains water-soluble when it is dry. It is a soft paint, which can be polished by burnishing to give a very smooth finish. It is available from art stores and some specialist paint suppliers. Apply it to a porous surface or over a coat of alcohol-based paint. Clean your brushes in water.

Several types of **ceramic paint** are available, and they can be either water- or oil-based. They are available from art stores and from many craft suppliers. Check before you buy, because some kinds have to be baked in the oven to make them set. Follow the manufacturer's instructions for use and for cleaning brushes.

Metal paints are very hard-wearing and will adhere to most surfaces. They are available in both spray and brush-on forms, although if you use spray paint, make sure you work in a well-ventilated room or, preferably, outdoors. Some types can be used to isolate rust, while other kinds should be applied only when the rust has been treated and isolated. When they are dry, they can be dissolved with denatured alcohol or the appropriate solvent, such as xylene, acetone or toluene, recommended by the manufacturer. Also follow the manufacturer's instructions for cleaning brushes.

Enamel paints, which are available in art stores, some craft suppliers and hardware stores, are oil-based and can be used on metal, glass, ceramics, plastics and wood. Dilute the paint with turpentine or mineral spirits, which should also be used for cleaning your brushes.

Acrylic varnish, which is water-based, is now widely available in places that sell other household paints. It is quick-drying and non-yellowing, and although it looks milky when you apply it, it dries clear. Check the durability before you buy because some are tougher than others. The varnish can be tinted with artists'

acrylics, gouache and universal stainers, which need to be diluted with water before they are added to the varnish. Some of the better brands will adhere to nonporous surfaces, but others need to be treated as latex paints. The varnish is waterproof when it is dry, but you should wash your brushes in water.

Shellac is available through specialist suppliers and some hardware stores. It comes in a wide variety of grades and stages of refinement, all of which are quick-drying, and it is also obtainable in flakes, which can be dissolved in denatured alcohol even when they are dry. Shellac button polish or sanding sealer should be used for the projects described in this book. Shellac can be used to seal bare wood, and it will adhere to most surfaces. It is often used to form an isolating layer between two incompatible paints. Wash brushes in denatured alcohol.

White polish, a more highly refined form of shellac, gives a transparent finish. It dissolves in denatured alcohol, even when it is dry, and you should clean your brushes in denatured alcohol. It is available from the same sources as other shellac products.

Oil-based varnish contains resins and oils that usually cause it to yellow as it ages. Normally the stronger the varnish – yacht varnish, for example – the more yellow it becomes. It is, however, very durable, waterproof, and widely available from stores selling household paints and varnishes. It will adhere to most surfaces and can be tinted with artists' oil paints, which should be diluted with mineral spirits before being added to the varnish. Clean your brushes in mineral spirits.

Crackle varnish, which is sometimes sold as cracklure, is a two-part product. The first, slow-drying coat continues to dry under the second, fast-drying coat, causing the top coat to crack. It can be unpredictable, and drying times vary considerably depending on the thickness of the coat, the circulation of air around the painted item, the humidity and so on. The varnish has to be patinated with artists' oil tube paints or powders to reveal the cracks to best effect. It is usually supplied as one oil-based and one water-based varnish, although wholly water-based versions are available. Brands that have an oil-based first coat can be used on most surfaces. Check the manufacturer's instructions before you begin. You will find crackle varnish in specialist paint stores and in some art stores.

Wax is widely available in clear form or in different wood colors. It is useful for antiquing surfaces, and it can also be tinted with artists' oil paints or with shoe polish. Wax should always be the final finish: do not attempt to varnish over it. Although the surface is waterproof, you will need to re-wax regularly. Use mineral spirits to clean your brushes.

Antiquing fluid can be bought ready-made, or you can mix your own with artists' oil paints and mineral spirits. The consistency can range from thick cream to a runny liquid. Earth colors – raw umber, burnt umber, green umber and Payne's gray, for example – are normally used.

Crackle varnish – first, oil-based coat

Crackle varnish – second, water-based coat

Oil-based varnish tinted with raw umber

Antique colored wax

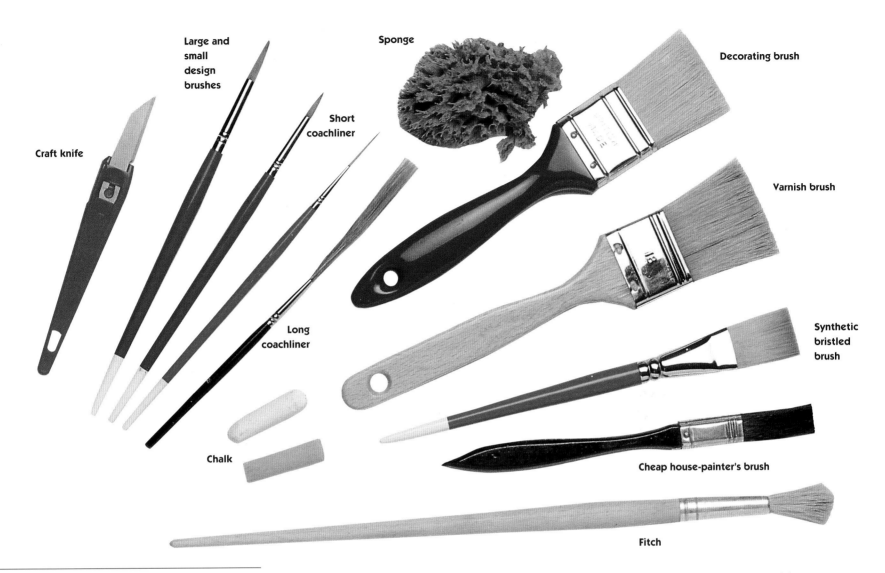

Craft knife

Large and small design brushes

Short coachliner

Sponge

Decorating brush

Varnish brush

Synthetic bristled brush

Long coachliner

Chalk

Cheap house-painter's brush

Fitch

BRUSHES

You will need a selection of brushes to complete the projects described in this book. The best brushes are expensive, but if you take care of them they will last for many years. Cheaper brushes are available, and if you are not intending to do a lot of painting, you may find they are adequate. Do not expect them to last, however. Always try to use the appropriate brush for the type of project and the paint you will be applying.

Varnish brushes are flat and are available in a variety of widths and kinds, ranging from pure bristle to synthetic fibers. When you apply water-based paints and varnishes, the synthetic brushes are generally better because they give a better flow and tend not to leave brush marks. They are not essential, however. You can use a varnish brush for paint as well as for varnish, especially when you are

decorating small items, but in general it is best to keep separate brushes for paint and for varnish and for oil- and water-based products.

House-painter's brushes have much thicker heads than varnish brushes, although they, too, are available in a variety of widths and types. When you are applying paint, use the largest brush you can, simply because it will give you quicker coverage. If you are planning to work on small articles only, you will probably not need a house-painter's brush, and a selection of varnish brushes will be sufficient. It is, however, worth buying one or two small, cheap brushes to use with shellac, because the denatured alcohol in it will ruin your brushes.

Fitches are used for oil painting, and they are available in art stores and some craft suppliers. They generally have long handles and short, stiff bristles, and they are made in various sizes and shapes. Fitches are useful for spattering and for mixing paints

and varnishes, but they are not essential.

Also available from art stores, **design brushes** are made in a choice of sizes and different kinds of hair. Really good brushes can be expensive, and if you are working with acrylics, it is better to use a synthetic brush. (In fact, top-quality sable watercolor brushes should not be used for any of the projects described in this book.) The most useful sizes to begin with are No. 4, No. 6 and No. 9.

Brushes known as **coachliners** are used for painting free-style lines. They look rather daunting, but they do make drawing lines easier. They have long hairs, all the same lengths, which are tear-shaped, so that the line is the same width throughout. They are available with long or short hairs and in a variety of widths. The short ones are for painting curves and short lines, and for the projects in this book you will find a short, No. 1 brush most useful.

OTHER EQUIPMENT

In addition to paints and a good selection of brushes, you will also use some or all of the following to complete the projects.

◊ Natural sponge: the frilly outer edge gives a varied pattern when it is used for sponging. Always squeeze out in water before use to soften the sponge and never leave it soaking in harsh solvents. Synthetic sponges are not a suitable substitute.

◊ Craft knife: these are always useful to have, and cheap, disposable ones are widely available. Dispose of used blades safely.

◊ Steel wool: you can buy a choice of grades. The finest, grade 0000, is used for burnishing.

◊ Sandpaper: you will use a variety of grades of ordinary sandpaper or of wet and dry paper.

◊ Chalk: blackboard chalk is useful for planning designs on furniture and other large items. Be careful if you use colored chalk because it may stain your work.

◊ Graphite tracing-down paper: wax-free paper is used to transfer designs to most surfaces, and it is easy to remove with a damp cloth. It is available in a variety of colors and is invaluable if you are going to trace a lot of designs. An alternative would be to use a soft pencil to outline the reverse of your design before tracing over the front with a sharp, hard pencil. Ordinary carbon paper is slightly waxy; it not only resists being painted over, but is likely to stain.

◊ Tracing paper: the see-through film is readily available and ideal for transferring designs.

◊ Drawing pens: most drawing pens have thin fiber tips, but you should test them before use to make sure that they will not smudge when varnished. For the projects used in this book you will need alcohol-proof pens, which are available from art stores and good stationery outlets.

Drawing pen

Pencil

Graphite tracing-down paper

Tracing paper

TECHNIQUES

PREPARING SURFACES

Bare Wood
Bare wood must be sealed, usually with an oil- or water-based priming paint or with shellac/sanding sealer. There are practically no limits to the paints or varnishes that can be used, and bare wood can be stained before sealing.

Varnished Wood
Before applying latex paint, sand the item with medium to coarse sandpaper to create a key to which the paint can adhere. If the sanding exposes a lot of bare wood, apply a coat of acrylic primer/undercoat or a coat of shellac/sanding sealer. Any types of paint or varnish can be used over the latex.

The surface must be sound before a coat of oil-based paint or varnish is applied. Flaking or loose varnish must be removed, and you will have to sand lightly with fine to medium-grade sandpaper to create a key for further coats of paint to cling to. Only oil- or alcohol-based products can be used over oil-based base coats.

Painted Wood
If something is already painted with a water-based finish, as long as the finish is sound, you can paint over it with any kind of paint you wish. If the existing paint is oil-based, it may still be possible to use a water-based paint, especially if the existing surface was applied some time ago, because the water-resistant oils will have tended to dry out. You may find that you need only give the surface a light sanding to provide a key for the new paint. You would also prepare the surface in this way if you were planning to use oil-based paint.

An alternative approach is to sand the surface lightly and then to apply an isolating coat of shellac, which is compatible with both oil- and water-based paints.

If the original coat is chipped, you must repair the chips with a primer. If the existing paint has been badly applied and has run, you will probably find it easier to strip the paint completely before you begin. There are several good commercial paint removers on the market – always read the manufacturer's directions before you begin – or, if the piece can be easily transported, have it stripped professionally.

Medium Density Fiberboard (MDF)
You should treat this composition material as you would ordinary wood.

Metal
Use a wire brush to remove any loose rust, and then use a rust remover to stop the metal from corroding further. Apply a coat of metal primer before giving a top coat of metal or oil-based paint.

Some paints are available that do most of this work for you, so all you need do is remove the loose flakes of rust. Follow the manufacturer's directions.

BRUSH STROKES

In the tradition of folk painting, most designs on painted furniture are very stylized. If you look at traditional Scandinavian, European and North American furniture and boat and cart painting, you will see that the designs tend to be built up with single brush-strokes. This style was not only quick to execute, but it gave a feeling of spontaneity and sense of movement that could never be achieved simply by coloring in shapes. It takes a little time and effort to master the technique, but it is well worth practicing on scrap paper before you begin.

Practice the movements described below until you get a feeling for how and when to twist the brush. For the strokes to look good, they will have to be done fairly quickly and in a single movement, but it may be helpful to work through the strokes in "slow motion" before you begin. The same rules apply whether you are left- or right-handed. The handle of the brush should always turn toward the inner edge of the curve, so for strokes facing the opposite way, turn the handle clockwise.

The brush strokes illustrated here are a guide only. If you master them, you will be able to paint easily and quickly every time. This is not, however, the only way to paint, and if you have a style and method with which you feel comfortable and achieve the results you want, that is fine. No two artists work in exactly the same way, and that is what makes this such an individual and challenging pastime.

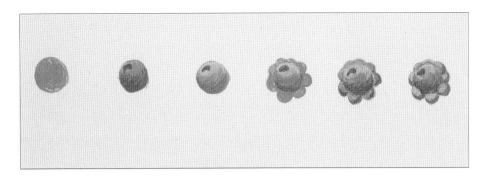

RIGHT: **Paint each rose from start to finish, keeping the paint wet to blend the colors**

Free-hand Lining

Use a coachliner or a sword liner because the length of the hairs will help you achieve a straight line that is the same width along its length. Load the whole brush, drawing it through the paint without twisting the hairs. Place the whole length of the brush down, just keeping the metal ferule clear of the surface. Always draw the brush toward you because your arm will naturally move in an arc if you paint from side to side. If you are painting close to an edge, place your little finger on the edge to support your hand and help to maintain a straight line. Always have a straight edge – a ruler, for example – about 1 inch from the line you are drawing so that your eye can use it as a guide, but never use a ruler to paint against. Small wobbles and uneven lines can be rectified by going over the line once it is dry. As you near the end of the line, begin to lift the brush. Keep a damp cloth on hand so that you can wipe off any mistakes.

Roses

Complete each rose before moving on to the next because the paint must be kept wet to blend the colors. Mix a light, medium and dark shade of the same color on your palette before starting. When you are painting anything that is to look three-dimensional, you must decide on the position of an imaginary light source and then be consistent in the placing of highlights and shadows. In the examples illustrated, the light source is from the top left-hand side.

Use the medium shade to paint a ball. Add shade to the lower right with the dark shade and make a dark dot in the top left to represent the heart of the flower. Add highlights to the top left with the lightest shade, then use the medium shade to paint the petals. Shade the petals at the bottom right of the rose before highlighting the petals on the top right and top left of the rose.

Curves and Petals

Use a round-ended design brush and press the whole brush down firmly, twisting it counterclockwise as you slide it sideways (**A**). Gradually lift the brush as you draw the arc, still twisting the hairs to give a clean point.

To paint a tear-shaped petal (**B**) use a round-ended design brush and push the brush down; then lift while turning the handle counterclockwise to bring the hairs to a fine point.

Use a pointed design brush to paint a curved line (**C**). Place only the tip of the brush on the surface, gradually pressing it down as you move the brush to increase the width of the stroke. Then twist the handle counterclockwise while pulling it up again to make a point.

Paint a leaf with two strokes of the brush (**D**). Work in the same way as for the tear-shaped stroke, but make a gentle S-shape. Make the second stroke as a tear next to the first.

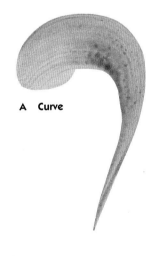

A   Curve

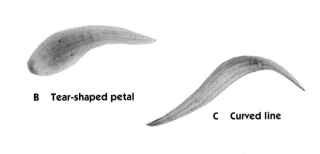

B   Tear-shaped petal

C   Curved line

D   Leaf

TOY BOX

This is a simple project to get you started, and it requires no special artistic skill to
complete. Remember that you want the box to look hand-painted, so do not worry unduly
if the lines are not absolutely straight. It will loose its charm if it looks machine-printed.

You will need

◊ Rectangular box – ours was 19 x 12 x 9 inches
◊ Acrylic primer/undercoat
◊ Sandpaper
◊ 1-inch flat varnish brush
◊ Latex paint – yellow
◊ Ruler and chalk
◊ Latex paint or artists' acrylics – pink and green
◊ Saucer or plate (for mixing paint)
◊ Coachliner
◊ Water-based varnish and varnish brush

1 Prepare the box. If the wood is untreated, seal it
with acrylic primer/undercoat and, when dry, sand
it lightly (see Preparing Surfaces, page 8). Apply a
coat of yellow latex and leave to dry. Find the
center of each side and mark it with chalk, then use
a small amount of pink and dilute with water. Use a
flat varnish brush to paint in the pink lines. Do not
overload the brush with paint and use the width of
the bristles to give the width of the lines. If you
prefer, draw in all the lines with chalk before you
begin.

TIP

• Always bring the brush toward you
when you are painting straight lines.
Tip the box toward you so that it is
balanced on its edge in your free
hand, and, while you pull the brush
toward you, slowly tip the box
backward. You will barely have to
move your arm and will achieve a
straight line much more easily.

• When you draw fine lines, you need
very little paint. Use trial-size cans
made by some paint manufacturers.
You will waste less paint, and they cost
less to buy than artists' acrylics.

2 Allow the pink paint to dry, then dilute the green
paint. Work in the same way, but at right angles to
the pink lines. The gap between the green lines
should be narrower than the gap between the pink
lines.

3 Use a coachliner and pink to paint two parallel
lines between the wide pink lines, then use green to
paint one line between the wide green lines. Finish
the outside of the box by painting the molded
edge with undiluted green latex. Give the inside a
coat of primer before applying green latex.

4

4 Cover the whole box with a coat of water-based varnish. Because the box may have to withstand a fair amount of wear and tear, use a durable floor varnish and apply three or four coats, allowing each coat to dry completely before you apply the next.

CANDLESTICKS

We gave these candlesticks the look of imitation Chinese lacquer, which is a simple way of decorating either wooden or papier-mâché candlesticks. We used new wooden ones, but you could give some old ones a new lease on life.

You will need
◊ Pair of wooden or papier-mâché candlesticks
◊ Shellac and small, inexpensive bristle brush
◊ Sandpaper
◊ Casein paint – black, Venetian red and gold
◊ Fine steel wool – grade 0000
◊ Denatured alcohol
◊ Brush (for applying paint)
◊ Artists' brush (for painting gold line)
◊ Clear furniture wax (optional)

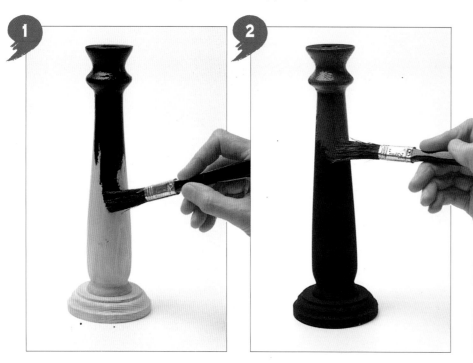

1 If you are renovating old candlesticks, see Preparing Surfaces (page 8) before you begin. Seal the candlesticks with a coat of shellac and leave to dry for about 15 minutes. If the candlesticks are wood, sand them lightly to remove any roughness caused where the grain has been raised. Apply three coats of black paint, allowing each coat to dry before applying the next.

2 Apply one coat of red paint and leave to dry.

TIP

• Although casein paint is water-based and will dry fairly quickly, each subsequent coat will take a little longer to dry than the one before.

3 Burnish vigorously with steel wool. This is like polishing and will not only reveal some of the underlying black, but will give the paint a high luster. Burnish all over once, then concentrate on small areas, especially those that would naturally become worn, such as raised moldings, to reveal more black.

TIP

• If you have difficulty in exposing the black paint when you are burnishing with steel wool, use a cloth dampened in a little water to dissolve the paint. Take great care, however, and use the cloth cautiously or you may expose the bare wood.

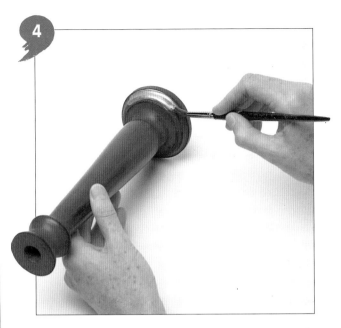

4 Pick out the moldings with gold paint, taking care not to go beyond the area of the moldings.

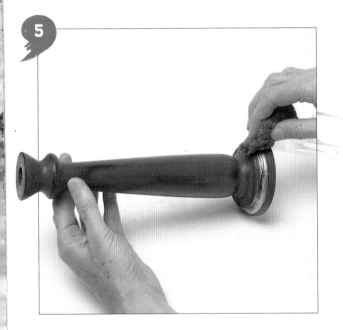

5 When the gold paint is dry, burnish it to reveal some of the underlying paint and to create an attractive luster. Although it is not essential, you can seal the finish to protect it with clear furniture wax.

WATERING CAN

This simple yet pretty watering can will brighten the chore of watering your indoor or conservatory plants. We chose a design based on motifs drawn from a manmade pond – goldfish and dragonflies – and the outlines are easily traced on and colored in, so no special artistic skills are required.

You will need

◊ Metal watering can
◊ Metal paint – blue (we used paint with a hammered finish)
◊ Brush for metal paint
◊ Solvent to clean brush (see manufacturer's directions)
◊ Tracing paper
◊ Graphite tracing-down paper
◊ Pencil
◊ Masking tape
◊ Artists' acrylic paints – white, cadmium red, cadmium yellow, phthalocyanine turquoise and phthalocyanine blue
◊ Saucer or plate (for mixing paint)
◊ Design brush – No. 4
◊ Varnish and varnish brush

1 Cover the watering can with a coat of metal paint. Some metal paints are very thick and form dribbles and runs while they dry. Keep your brush handy and watch the can until the paint is dry.

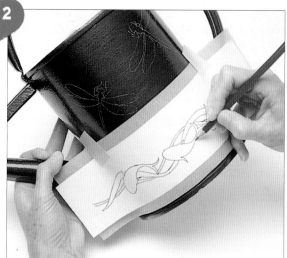

2 Transfer the fish design (see page 48) to tracing paper and place the paper around the bottom edge of the can, using masking tape to hold it in position. Insert the tracing-down paper and use a sharp pencil to go over the design. Copy and transfer the dragonflies (see page 48) in the same way.

3 Use two shades of acrylic blue to paint the wavy lines between the fish to suggest water.

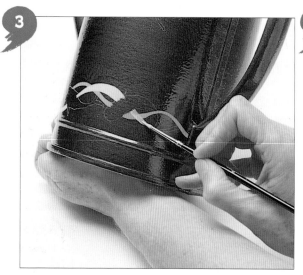

4 Mix red and yellow to give a rich orange color and paint in the goldfish. Highlight the top edge of each fish with a fine yellow line.

5 Block in the dragonflies with white paint. This is necessary because the background color is dark, and they would not otherwise show up.

6 Allow the white paint to dry before applying a wash of turquoise. Simply mixing turquoise and white would have given a pastel shade, but overpainting the turquoise on white gives a vibrant color.

7 Decorate the edges and spout of the watering can with wavy lines, painted in orange to echo the color of the fish.

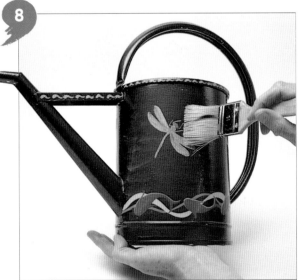

8 Give the watering can several coats of varnish, allowing each to dry before you apply the next.

TIP
• Some of the solvents recommended for cleaning brushes used for metal paints are very expensive. You may find it more economical to use a cheaper brush and discard it after use.

MIRROR FRAME

This pen-work frame looks like inlaid wood, but the intricacy of the design belies its simplicity, for the motifs are traced on and painted around. Choose a frame that is made of light wood and that has a simple profile.

You will need

◊ Wooden frame
◊ Ruler and pencil
◊ Shellac and cheap house-painter's brush
◊ Sandpaper
◊ Tracing paper
◊ Graphite tracing-down paper
◊ Masking tape
◊ Alcohol-proof drawing pen
◊ Small design brush
◊ Artists' acrylic paint – black
◊ Denatured alcohol (to clean brush)
◊ White polish
◊ Fine steel wool – grade 0000

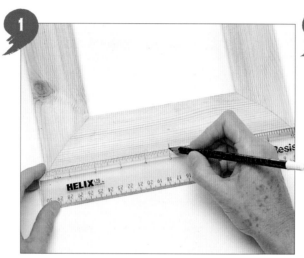

1 Use a ruler and pencil to mark the center of each side of the frame.

2 Apply a coat of shellac to the frame to seal the wood. When it is dry, lightly sand the frame to remove the roughness of the raised grain.

3 Transfer the motif (see page 48) to tracing paper and position it centrally along the side of the frame, using the marks made in step 1 as your guide. Hold the tracing in place with masking tape and slide the tracing-down paper under it. Use a sharp pencil to go over the outlines.

4

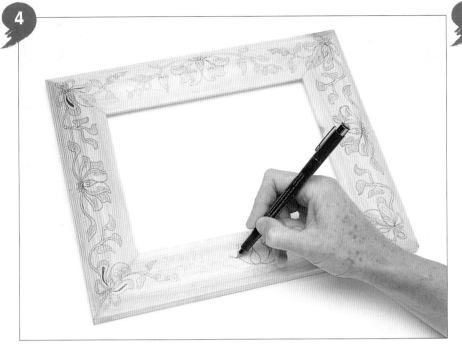

4 Go over the traced lines with a drawing pen. You may need to adjust the position of the corner motifs if your frame is a different size from the one we used. Alternatively, add leaves or make the stems longer so that the design will fit, but make sure that you keep the overall proportions the same. You may want to redraw the motifs onto clean tracing paper before transferring the outlines to the frame.

5

5 Using a small design brush and black acrylic paint, carefully block in the background so that the design shows in relief. You will probably need two coats to give good coverage, so remember to allow the first coat to dry before applying the second.

6

6 When the whole frame is painted and completely dry, apply a coat of white polish. Leave to dry for about 15 minutes.

7

7 Gently burnish the frame with steel wool to give a smooth finish. Apply several coats of white polish, allowing each to dry before burnishing. Do not burnish the final coat.

TRAY

Naive art has a wonderfully refreshing simplicity. The style was originally used to record events and objects that were important in everyday life, and because the paintings were not executed by great artists, they have a beguiling and often humorous charm. Prize livestock was a popular subject and is appropriate for a kitchen tray. We chose a sheep and finished the design with some free-hand lines.

You will need

◊ Tray (ours was wooden; if you use a different kind of tray, turn to Preparing Surfaces, page 8, before you begin)
◊ Shellac and brush
◊ Fine sandpaper
◊ Latex paint – dark blue-green
◊ Tracing paper
◊ Pencil
◊ Masking tape
◊ Graphite tracing-down paper
◊ Artists' acrylic paints – white, raw umber and black
◊ Design brushes – No. 8 or 9 and No. 4
◊ Saucer or plate (for mixing paint)
◊ Short coachliner
◊ Varnish and varnish brush

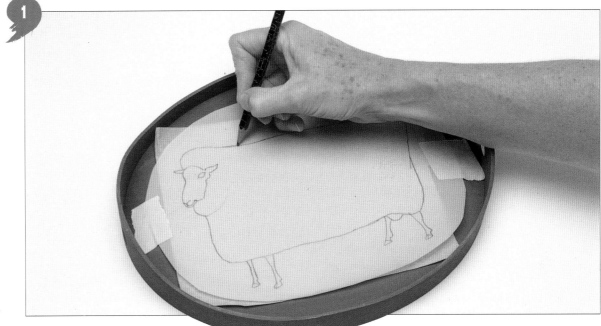

1 Seal the tray with a coat of shellac. Sand it lightly to smooth the surface before applying a coat of blue-green latex. Transfer the design (see page 48) to tracing paper, hold it in position with masking tape, and use tracing-down paper to transfer the outline to the tray.

2 Mix white acrylic paint with a little raw umber in a saucer or plate to create an off-white color and use it to block in the sheep's body. Because the background is dark, you will probably not achieve a perfect cover with one coat.

3 When the first coat of paint is dry, use the same off-white to stipple on a second coat very thickly to give the texture and impression of fleece.

4 Add more raw umber to the original color and shade the sheep's body, adding shadow to the belly, along the back, and around the neck to create a three-dimensional effect.

5 Use raw umber mixed with a little white to paint the details of the face – eyes, nose and ears – and to add more shadow under the chin. Use black acrylic for the pupils of the eyes and for the legs.

6 Add a sparkle to the eyes and highlights to the hooves with white acrylic paint.

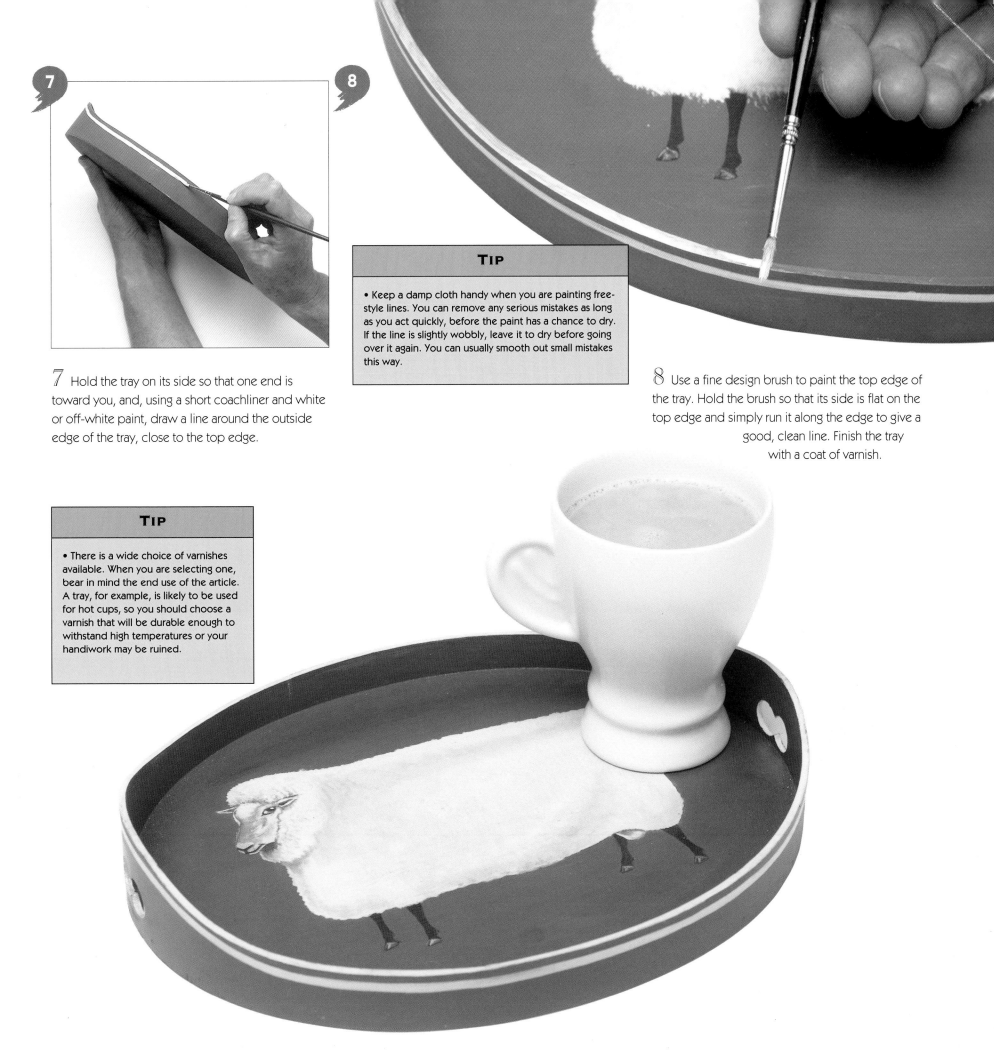

7 Hold the tray on its side so that one end is toward you, and, using a short coachliner and white or off-white paint, draw a line around the outside edge of the tray, close to the top edge.

TIP

• Keep a damp cloth handy when you are painting free-style lines. You can remove any serious mistakes as long as you act quickly, before the paint has a chance to dry. If the line is slightly wobbly, leave it to dry before going over it again. You can usually smooth out small mistakes this way.

8 Use a fine design brush to paint the top edge of the tray. Hold the brush so that its side is flat on the top edge and simply run it along the edge to give a good, clean line. Finish the tray with a coat of varnish.

TIP

• There is a wide choice of varnishes available. When you are selecting one, bear in mind the end use of the article. A tray, for example, is likely to be used for hot cups, so you should choose a varnish that will be durable enough to withstand high temperatures or your handiwork may be ruined.

CHAIR

Most of us have pieces of furniture that have seen better days, but that we would be sad to part with. As long as the underlying shape is attractive, there are all kinds of ways in which we can turn these battered items into beautiful objects. The finish described here would suit a period setting and would blend in well with other antiques.

You will need

◊ Chair
◊ Coarse sandpaper
◊ Acrylic primer/undercoat
◊ House-painter's brush – 1–1½ inches
◊ Latex paint – white and dark blue-green
◊ Denatured alcohol
◊ Paper towels or old cloth
◊ Chalk
◊ Tracing paper
◊ Pencil
◊ Graphite tracing-down paper
◊ Masking tape
◊ Artists' acrylic paints – Hooker's green, phthalocyanine blue and white
◊ Saucer or plate (for mixing paint)
◊ Design brush – No. 4
◊ Varnish and varnish brush

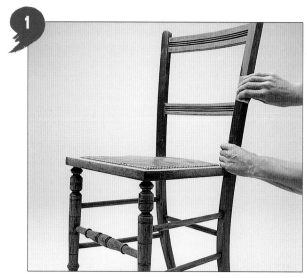

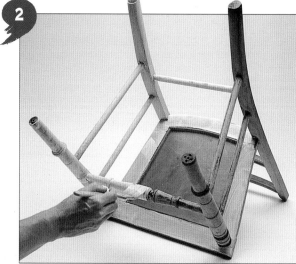

1 This worn and scuffed chair still had the remains of its original varnish, which, because of the chair's age, would probably have been shellac. Because the chair will receive several coats of paint, use coarse sandpaper to remove the old finish. Work outside if possible because this is a messy job; if you have to work indoors, wear a face mask and make sure that your working area is well ventilated.

2 When the chair is back to the bare wood, seal it with acrylic primer or undercoat. Begin by painting the legs and support rails, then paint around the turned rails. If the legs are not turned, follow the grain of the wood and paint up and down. The chair can then be turned the right way up and the top half painted.

3 Apply three coats of white latex, allowing each coat to dry completely before adding the next. Paint as neatly as you can because the brush marks will show when the chair is finished. When the white latex is dry, apply a coat of dark blue-green latex diluted in the proportions of 1 part paint to 5 parts water. Leave to dry.

4 Wet some paper towels or an old rag with denatured alcohol and carefully rub over the chair, working on one section at a time. Denatured alcohol is a solvent for dry latex paint, so work carefully because it will remove not only the pale blue-green, but may also take off enough white to reveal the wood underneath. You are aiming for a grainy look with the blue-green sitting in the brush marks and the white showing through.

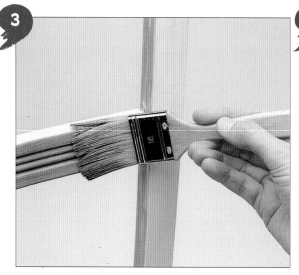

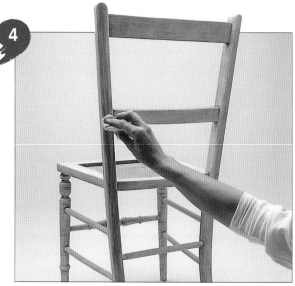

5

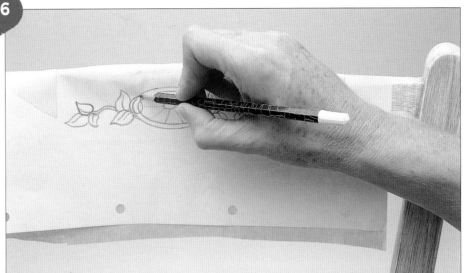

6

5 On all turned areas, moldings or carvings, rub across the indentations so that the blue-green is not removed and the crevices remain quite dark. On raised areas, remove more of the blue-green so that they appear lighter than the main body of the chair. This will help to highlight the details of the chair's shape.

6 Use chalk to mark the center of the back rail. Transfer the design (see page 48) to tracing paper and place it centrally on the back rail, holding it in place with masking tape. Use tracing-down paper and a sharp pencil to transfer the design to the chair.

8

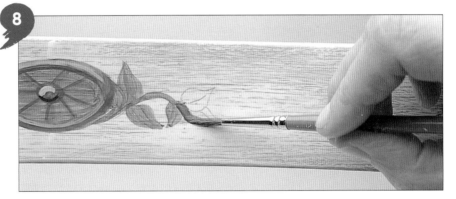

7

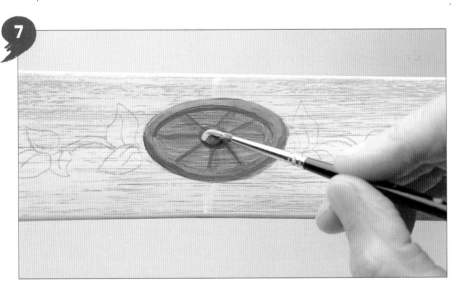

9

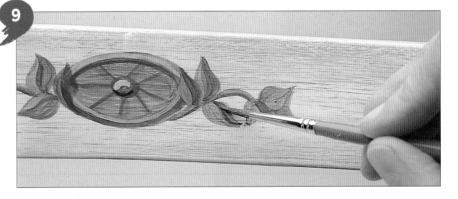

7 Mix the green and blue acrylic paints with a little white and use them to block in the central oval. To give the design depth, it needs to be shaded and highlighted. Decide on an imaginary source of light and use darker green to add shade. We assumed that light was coming from the top left and added shade under the oval, on the right-hand side of the curve and the top left-hand side of the inner curve, where the imagined roundness of the outside molding of the oval would have cast a shadow. Paint dark lines radiating from the center to the inner edge. Mix more white into the original color and highlight the facets that face the light source – in our case, this was the top left-hand side, the bottom right inner edge of the oval, and the left-hand side of the central oval.

8 Use a slightly greener shade to block in the stems and leaves at the sides of the oval.

9 With an even darker green, shade the leaves, observing the same imagined light source as in step 7. Also add shade to the underside of the stem by painting in a thin dark green line.

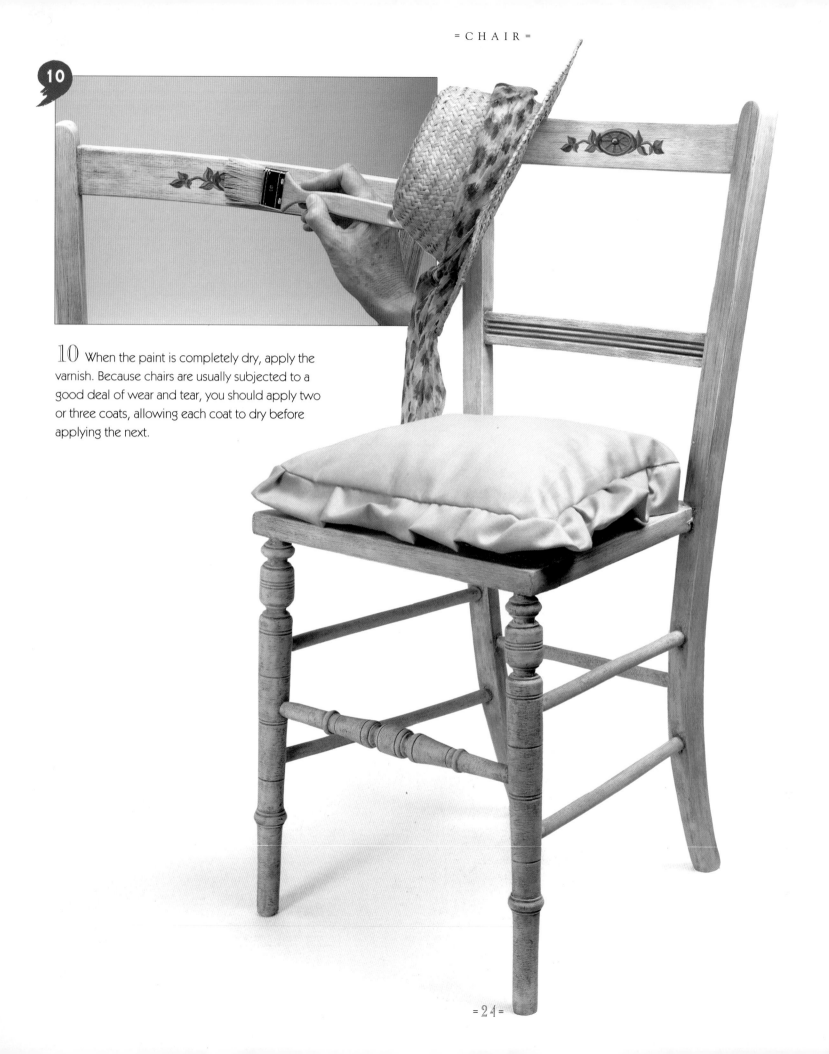

10

10 When the paint is completely dry, apply the varnish. Because chairs are usually subjected to a good deal of wear and tear, you should apply two or three coats, allowing each coat to dry before applying the next.

BOOK-SHAPED BOX

It's always good to be able to personalize items, especially if you are going to give them as gifts. This box was already shaped like a book, which made us think of an illuminated initial letter, but that would have limited the use of the design. The pattern is, therefore, one in which different initials can be inserted. It is possible to find books with different styles of lettering, which you can adapt as you wish.

You will need

◊ Box
◊ Shellac or acrylic primer/undercoat
◊ Brush for shellac
◊ Sandpaper
◊ Latex paint – blue
◊ 1-inch brush
◊ Latex or artists' acrylic paint – white, blue, yellow, Venetian red, black and Hooker's green
◊ Saucer or plate (for mixing paint)
◊ Natural sponge
◊ Small stiff-bristled brush such as a fitch
◊ Pencil and ruler
◊ Short coachliner
◊ Tracing paper
◊ Masking tape
◊ Graphite tracing-down paper
◊ Design brush – No. 4
◊ Varnish and varnish brush

1 Seal the box with acrylic primer/undercoat and sand it lightly when dry. Apply a coat of blue latex, then mix two shades of blue, one lighter and one darker than your base color, diluting each with approximately 5 parts of water. Use a brush to put some paint on the dampened sponge. Do not dip the sponge in the paint or you will overload it.

2 Use a light dabbing movement to sponge the surface of the box. From time to time, turn the sponge in mid-air (not on the surface of the box) so that the pattern is varied. Repeat with the second color, filling in any spaces.

3 Mix another shade of blue (or a completely different color if you prefer) and use a stiff-bristled brush to spatter the surface, running your finger through the bristles to make tiny speckles.

4

5

6

4 Use a ruler and pencil to mark on the front of the box a rectangle that is about 1 inch smaller all around than the box. Paint this area yellow and leave it to dry. Then paint it red, diluting the paint a little to allow the yellow to show through. Paint carefully so that the brush marks do not show.

5 Use the coachliner to outline the rectangle with green paint, then paint another green line, about ⅛ inch outside the rectangle. Between the two green lines, paint two yellow lines, leaving blue showing between them.

6 Trace the lettering, using the outlines on page 48 if you wish, and position them so that they are centered near the top of the box. Hold it in place with masking tape and use tracing-down paper to transfer the letters. Do the same with the initials of your choice.

7

8

7 Block in the letters in black using a small, fine brush.

8 Highlight the letters with yellow before varnishing the box to protect it.

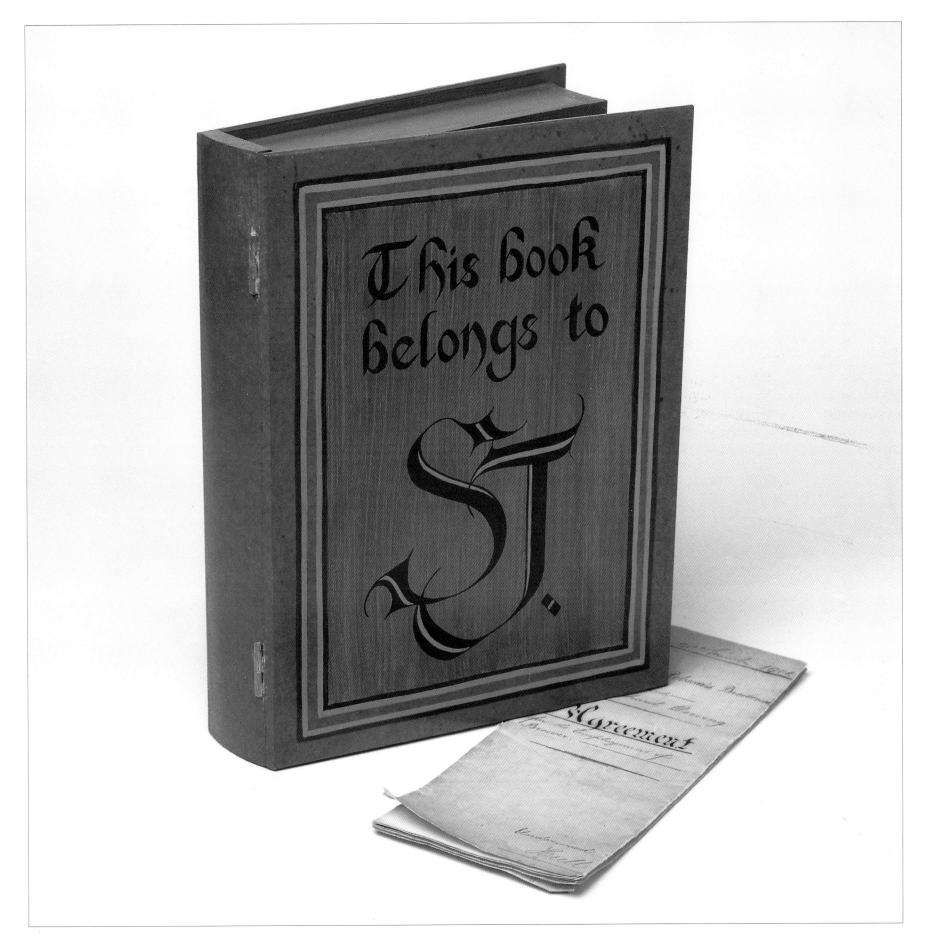

KITCHEN TILES

Hand-painted ceramic tiles can be very expensive, but it is possible to create your own, and each tile will be subtly different, which is part of their beauty. These tiles will never be as durable as tiles that have been glazed and fired after painting, and they are not, therefore, suitable for areas where they will receive heavy wear, but with care they will last for many years.

You will need

◊ Plain ceramic tiles
   (we used ones with a mottled finish)
◊ Short coachliner
◊ Ceramic paint
◊ Solvent (see manufacturer's
   guidance on paint can)
◊ Design brush – No. 4
◊ Tracing paper (optional)
◊ Pencil (optional)
◊ Masking tape (optional)
◊ Graphite tracing-down paper (optional)

1 Use a short coachliner to paint two parallel lines at the top and bottom of each tile, ¼ to ⅛ inch from the edge. When you have painted the first tile, lay the second next to it so that the lines will be continuous when the tiles are set in position.

TIP
• Once you have completed one tile, rest the next tile on top of it so that the border motif is just visible. You will then be able to copy the position of the motifs from one tile to the next without having to measure each one.

2 Begin in the top left-hand corner of the tile and measure the pattern so that the repeated motifs will be evenly spaced to coincide with the pattern on the neighboring tile. Use a small design brush to make three small, tear-shaped stroke along the outer border (see Brush Strokes, page 9). Make a small dot with the tip of the brush between each motif.

3 Use the tip of a short coachliner or a fine design brush to paint the outline of the bird. If you do not feel confident about painting it freestyle, trace a suitable design from a book and transfer it to the tile with graphite tracing-down paper.

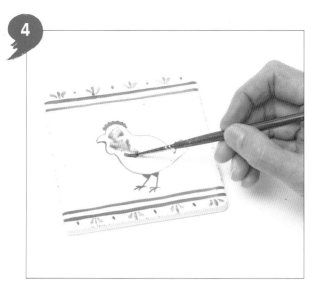

4 Leave the outline to dry. Dilute the paint according to the manufacturer's directions and fill in the shape.

5 Use a fine brush to paint in the details – eyes, wings, tail feathers and beak. Follow the manufacturer's recommendations for drying. If the paint does not need to be baked in an oven, leave it for at least 24 hours before setting the tiles into place because even if the paint feels dry, it will take time to cure thoroughly.

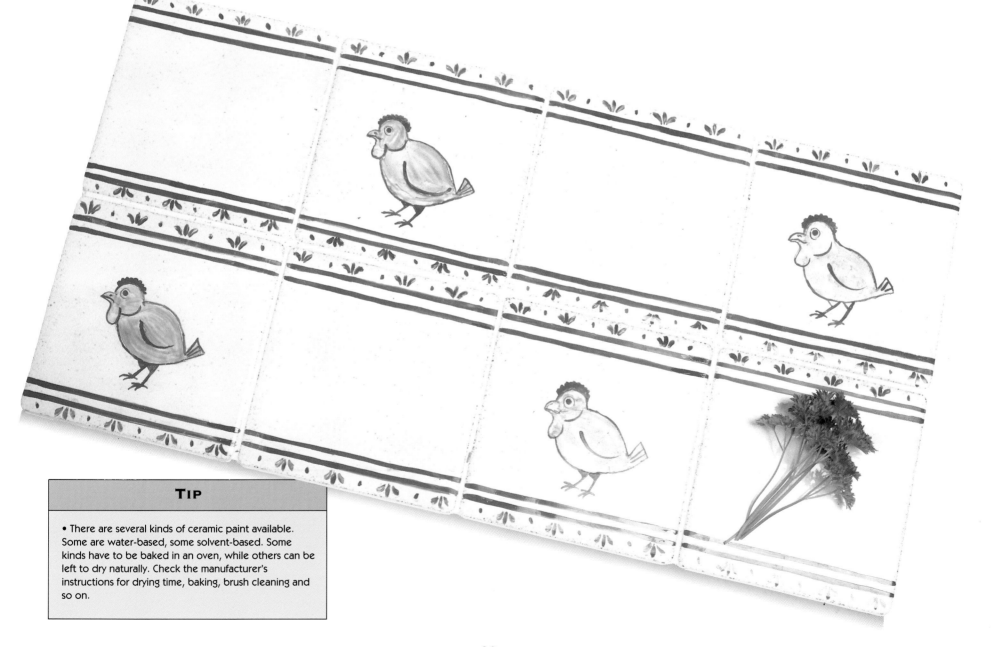

TIP

• There are several kinds of ceramic paint available. Some are water-based, some solvent-based. Some kinds have to be baked in an oven, while others can be left to dry naturally. Check the manufacturer's instructions for drying time, baking, brush cleaning and so on.

COMMEMORATIVE PLATE

A hand-painted plate to mark a special occasion is a wonderfully personal way to show that you have thought about the event. You could use the same basic idea to make a house-warming gift, when you might replace the child's name with the new address. We have used an inexpensive enamel plate and based the design on traditional bargeware. The same technique could be used on other enamel items.

You will need
◊ White enamel plate
◊ Colored chalk
◊ Enamel craft paints – red, white, light green and dark green
◊ Design brush – No. 4
◊ Mineral spirits (for cleaning brush)

1 Use chalk to indicate the position of the letters of the name, making sure they are evenly spaced. Paint the name in light green paint.

2 Shade the letters with dark green, remembering that you must determine your imaginary light source. In our example, the light source was from the top left-hand side, and the shading was, therefore, applied to the right-hand side and the bottom of the letters.

3 Sketch the central motif with chalk, indicating the positions of the leaves and main branch. If you want to use traditional roses, see Brush Strokes (page 9). Use light green to block in the leaves.

4 Shade the leaves to give a three-dimensional appearance, again bearing the imaginary light source in mind as you work. Mix a little red with the green to create a brown for the branch.

TIP

• Enamel items decorated in this way will withstand occasional gentle washing, but they are not suitable for everyday use.

5 Load the brush with red and drop paint onto the plate to form round blobs to represent the berries. Take care not to overload your brush, and test the amount of paint you need on the side of the plate. You can wipe it off with a paper towel soaked in mineral spirits before it dries.

6 Allow the berries to dry a little, then paint in the highlights with white paint to make them look round and shiny.

7 Hold the plate so that the name is at the top and find the center of the bottom. Allow enough room for the word and date, chalking the characters in so that they are evenly and symmetrically placed. Paint in the letters and numbers.

8 Paint a line around the border in red. Most enamel plates already have a blue edge, and you can paint over this. Leave the paint to dry for about 24 hours, although it will be dry to the touch after about 6 hours.

CLOCK FACE

A piece of medium-density fiberboard (MDF) was used for the face, and battery-operated hands are widely available in various styles. Although it looks complicated, the ship design is traced, and the central compass is drawn with ruler and compasses. Perhaps the most difficult feature are the freestyle lines; you should practice these on scrap paper before you begin. The face has been given an "antique" finish by a final coat of two-stage crackle varnish.

You will need

◊ Clockface and hands and movement
◊ Acrylic primer/undercoat
◊ Sandpaper
◊ Brushes for base coat and varnish –
   1–1⅛ inches
◊ Latex paint – yellow
◊ Square of cardboard, 10 x 10 inches
◊ School compass
◊ Ruler and pencil
◊ Protractor
◊ Scissors
◊ Artists' acrylic paint – Payne's gray,
   raw sienna, Venetian red and white
◊ Design brush – No. 4
◊ Short coachliner – No. 1
◊ Tracing paper
◊ Masking tape
◊ Graphite tracing-down paper
◊ Crackle varnish (optional)
◊ Oil-based varnish
◊ Artists' oil paint – raw umber
◊ Mineral spirits

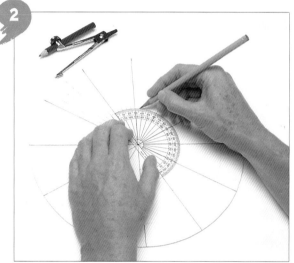

1 Seal the board with a coat of acrylic primer/undercoat and, when it is dry, sand it lightly. Apply a coat of yellow latex paint. If you prefer, use two coats of latex only, sanding between each one.

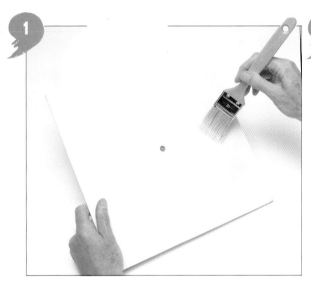

2 Use a school compass to draw a circle, 10 inches in diameter on the cardboard. Draw a line through the center of the circle, place the protractor on the line and mark sections every 30 degrees. Join the marks across the center to make 12 sections. Subdivide some of the sections by marking 6 degrees to give the minutes. Cut out the cardboard.

3 Measure and mark the central points of each side of the clock face. Position the cardboard dial centrally on the clock face, making sure that the points that will be 3, 6, 9 and 12 o'clock are correctly aligned. Draw around the cardboard circle and transfer the hour and minute measurements to the clock face.

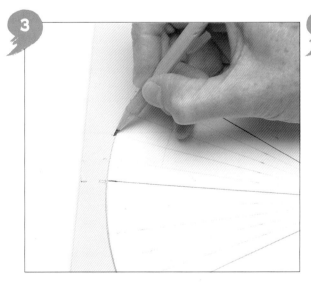

4 Use Payne's gray and a short coachliner to paint the circle. Paint a second circle, about ⅛ inch outside the first, and between the two circles paint in the minute and hour marks, differentiating between the two.

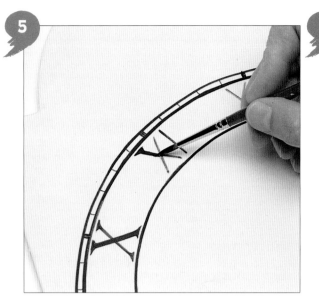

5 Draw the numerals with a pencil before painting them in. Make the line starting at the top left of the Xs and Vs as thick as the upright line of the Is, while the lines starting at the top right should be finer.

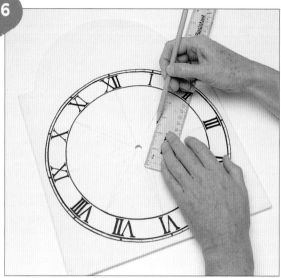

6 In the center of the dial draw a pencil line running horizontally from 9 to 3 and a vertical line running from 12 to 6. Place your protractor at the intersection of these lines and mark 45 degrees between each line. Join these points through the center. Find a point about 1 inch from the center on each of these lines and join this point to the top of the adjacent lines to form an eight-pointed star.

7 Use raw sienna to paint the star compass, diluting the paint with water to make the first coat fairly light. Use a stronger tone of the same color to add shade, remembering to identify the imaginary light source before you do so. We assumed a light source at the top left, so the two sections facing the light at 11 o'clock were left pale, while the two opposite section were shaded. The remaining sections alternated between light and dark.

8 With a coachliner and raw sienna, paint another circle outside the dial. Outline the whole clock face, too, following the arc at the top and joining the lines between the top corners.

9 Trace the ship and shooting star motifs (see page 48) and use tracing-down paper to transfer them to the clock face. Paint in the shooting stars in each corner, making the stars darker than the tails.

10 Use diluted raw sienna to paint in the ship, moon and sun. Paint the sails in white and add shadows with a little Payne's gray.

11 Mix a little Venetian red into the raw sienna and make the paint a little thicker before adding the details of the windows and so on, and to add more shadows to the ship. Leave the paint to dry.

12 If you do not want a crackle finish, apply a coat of varnish. If you use crackle varnish, apply the oil-based coat first. Use the varnish sparingly, spreading it out from the center before reloading your brush. Leave it to become tacky, which can take from 1 to 4 hours.

13 Test the varnish by pressing it lightly with your fingers. If should feel almost dry, but your fingers will feel a slight stickiness. Apply the second, water-based coat, which will dry fairly quickly. Make sure that the second coat covers the whole surface. While this coat is still wet, massage it lightly with your fingers to encourage it to adhere to the first coat. Stop massaging when the varnish begins to pull against your fingers and feels almost dry.

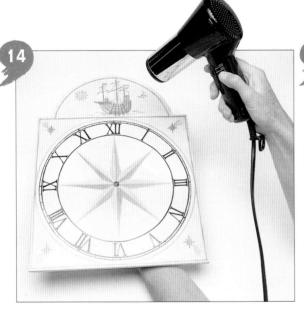

14 Leave to dry for at least 30 minutes, but preferably overnight. The second coat of varnish is water soluble, so take care that it does not come into contact with water and that you do not leave it in a damp atmosphere. Apply gentle heat to encourage the varnish to crack – you should be able to see the cracks when you hold the clock face up to the light.

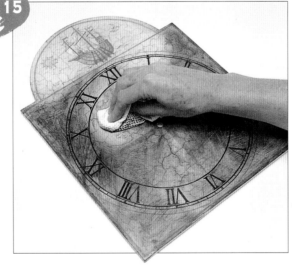

15 To patinate the clock face, squeeze about ½ inch of oil paint onto the surface. Do not use acrylic paint, which will remove the finish. Dampen a paper towel with a little mineral spirits and use a circular motion to spread the paint over the whole clock face and to encourage it into the cracks. Use a clean piece of paper towel to wipe off any excess.

TIP

• If the crackle varnish does not turn out as you hoped, remove the top, water-based coat by washing it off. You can then start again with the first coat of varnish without damaging the underlying painting.

16 Different pigments in oil paints dry at different rates. Raw umber dries in about 24 hours, but some colors take longer. When you are sure that the paint it dry, seal the surface with an oil-based varnish.

GAME BOARD

This could be the ideal present for someone who has everything. The board was cut from a piece of medium-density fiberboard (MDF), although the same idea could be used to decorate a table top.

You will need

◊ Square of MDF, 18 x 18 inches, or a suitable table
◊ Shellac and brush
◊ Denatured alcohol (to clean brush)
◊ Sandpaper
◊ Latex paint – dark red
◊ House-painter's brush
◊ Long ruler and pencil
◊ Artists' acrylic paints – black, gold, burnt umber and raw sienna
◊ Design brush – No. 8 or 9
◊ Coachliner
◊ Chalk
◊ Varnish and varnish brush
◊ Black felt and all-purpose adhesive to back board
◊ Craft knife

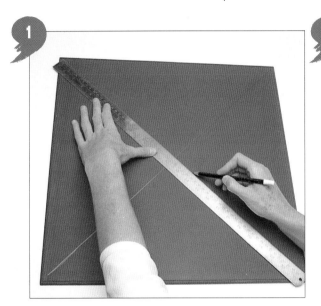

1 Prepare the board by sealing it with a coat of shellac. When it is dry, sand it and apply a coat of dark red latex. Leave to dry. Find the center of the board by drawing two diagonal lines.

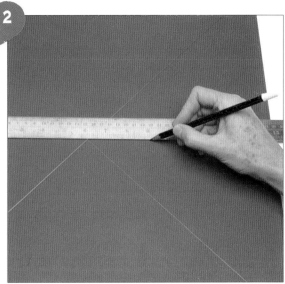

2 Measure from the intersection of the two diagonals the eight by eight squares needed for the standard game board.

TIP

• The project requires some skill with the paintbrush, and you should practice the brush strokes on scrap paper before you begin.

3 Mark the positions for the 64 squares. Our squares measured 1½ inches, giving an overall area of 12 x 12 inches.

4 Check that the width of the outside border is the same on all sides before drawing the squares.

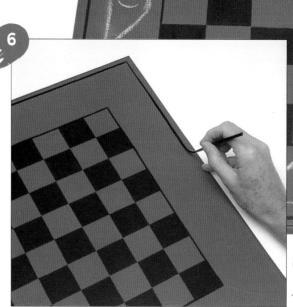

5 Use black acrylic paint to color alternate squares. Because it is so easy to go over a line, begin with your brush inside the line, move it up to the line, and draw it in again before you lift it from the surface.

6 Use a coachliner and black acrylic to paint a line around the squares and just inside the edge of the board.

7 Draw a chalk line about ⅛ inch in from the outer border and, working from the center, draw in symmetrical wavy lines, using the chalk line as a guide for the base of the wavy lines.

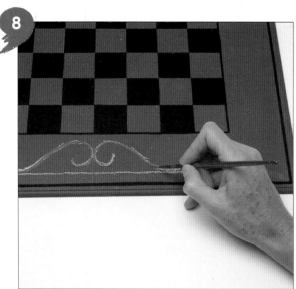

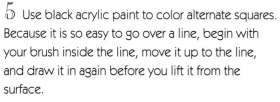

8 Use a fine design brush or short coachliner to paint over the wavy chalk lines with raw sienna. When the paint is dry, wipe away the straight chalk lines with a damp cloth.

9 Use a single stroke to chalk in the leaves, positioning them so that they grow from the center toward the corners. Vary the size of the leaves for interest. Paint the leaves in raw sienna with a single stroke (see Brush Strokes, page 8).

10 Go over the design painted in raw sienna in gold acrylic paint, again using single brush strokes for the leaves. Going over the pattern twice will make sure that it stands out against the dark background.

TIP

- If you have difficulty finding shellac, use two coats of latex paint, sanding the surface lightly between coats.

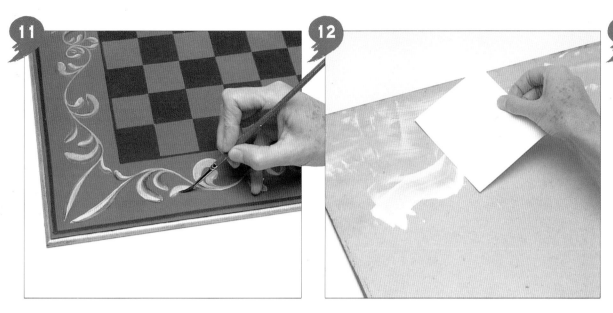

11 Use burnt umber to shade the design, remembering to make the shadows consistent with a single imagined light source. When the paint is dry, apply two or three coats of varnish.

12 If you have made a board, coat the underside with an even layer of all-purpose adhesive, using a small piece of cardboard to spread the glue, and place the felt over it, smoothing it down.

13 Turn over the board and use a craft knife to trim away the excess felt.

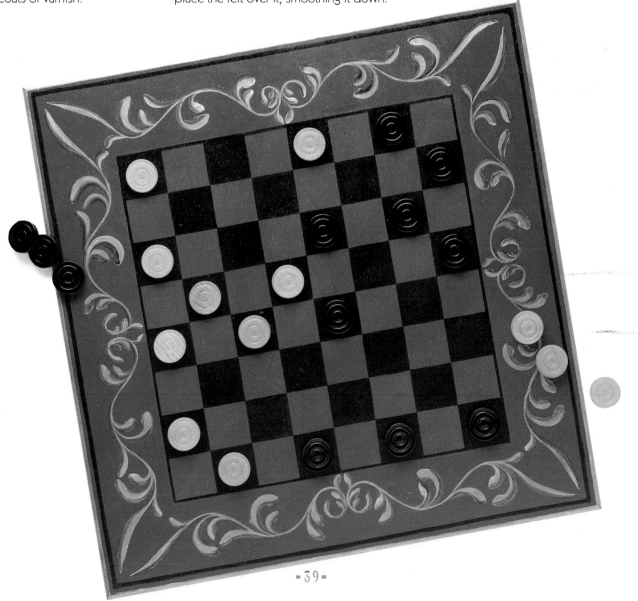

FIRESCREEN

The only difficult aspect of decorating this firescreen is drawing the outline of the potted auriculas. If you do not feel confident about your ability to draw a suitable motif freestyle, trace a design, using a photocopier or the grid method to enlarge an illustration that you like to the appropriate size. You can, of course, use colors that will harmonize with your own color scheme.

You will need
◊ Firescreen
◊ Acrylic primer/undercoat
◊ Brushes for primer and latex
◊ Sandpaper
◊ Latex paint – pale green
◊ Chalk
◊ Artists' acrylic paints – white, Hooker's green, Venetian red and cadmium yellow
◊ Saucer or plate (for mixing paint)
◊ Design brushes – No. 9 and No. 4
◊ Varnish and varnish brush
◊ Antique brown furniture wax

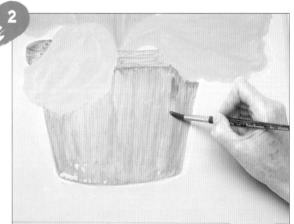

1 Seal the firescreen with acrylic primer/undercoat and sand lightly when it is dry. Apply a coat of pale green paint, leave to dry and then use chalk to draw in the outline of your design. Mix green and white acrylic paint and use the resulting pale green to block in the leaves and stems.

2 Use well-diluted Venetian red to paint the flowerpot. Use a thicker mix of the same color to add shadows under the rim and at the right-hand side of the pot.

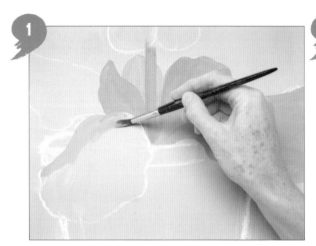

TIP

• If the green you mix to paint in the leaves and stems of your design is not a strong enough contrast to the background color, add a little red or blue to deepen the tone.

3 Paint in the veins and shadows of the leaves with Hooker's green.

4 Define the edges of the leaves with a fine white line.

5 Block in the flowers with white paint and pick out the edges of the petals with pink mixed from red and white. Work from the base of the pink section, blending in a darker shade of red but leaving the tips of the petals pale. Color the center of each flower with a small yellow circle and paint red lines radiating from it to the edge of each petal.

6 To give the flower head some depth, try to give the impression of flowers behind flowers by painting some in a darker shade of red.

7 If your screen has a molded edge, pick out the line in red.

8 Use colored wax to give an "antique" look. Rub the wax all over the surface, leave it to dry, then buff it with a soft cloth. If you wish, seal the screen with varnish before applying the wax to give extra protection.

CHEST OF DRAWERS

This miniature chest of drawers has been prettily decorated so that it is perfect for storing jewelry or all the other odds and ends that otherwise accumulate on a dresser. This method could be used to decorate a full-size chest of drawers, and the same design could be scaled up to make it appropriate for a larger piece of furniture.

You will need
◊ Miniature chest of drawers
◊ Acrylic primer/undercoat
◊ House-painter's brush
◊ Sandpaper
◊ Latex paint – turquoise
◊ Chalk
◊ Artists acrylic paints – Hooker's green, cadmium red, cadmium yellow and white
◊ Design brush – No. 4
◊ Antiquing fluid (use raw umber artists' oil paint mixed with mineral spirits to give a runny consistency)
◊ Oil-based varnish and varnish brush

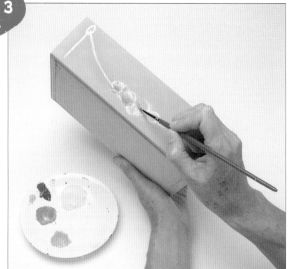

1 Seal the chest of drawers with acrylic primer/undercoat and sand lightly when it is dry. Apply a coat of turquoise latex. So that the drawers do not stick, do not paint the inside, but take the paint just around the top and sides of the drawers and just inside the drawer openings.

2 Replace the drawers and mark the design in chalk on the front, aligning the drops of the garlands on each drawer. Indicate the positions of the roses by simply drawing circles. Do not worry about the leaves at this stage.

3 Paint the roses one by one because the paint must be wet to allow you to blend in the colors (see Brush Strokes, page 9). Mix three shades of coral pink with the red, yellow and white. When you paint the roses, remember to apply shadow consistently.

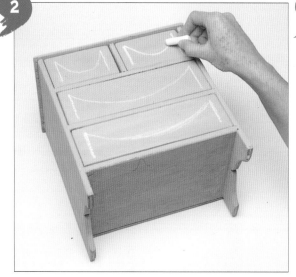

4

4 Paint the rosebuds by making a small oval with coral paint. Then use green to paint the sepals around the bud. Starting at the stem end, push the brush down and then up to form the sepals so that they are thick at the base and taper to a point.

5

5 Paint the leaves so that they just peep from behind the roses. Shade them on one side, using the same imagined light source as for the roses. Keep the design balanced, filling in any obvious gaps with leaves.

6

6 Paint in the stems for the garland and drops with green. The garland should emerge from the roses at a point just above the center so that it looks as if it is supporting the roses.

7

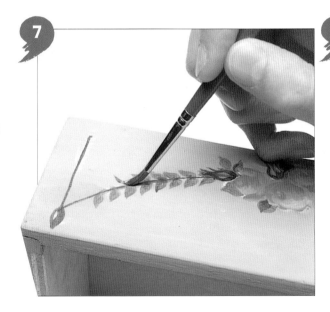

7 Paint in the leaves along the garland (see Brush Strokes, page 9), remembering to make them look as if they are growing from the center out. The leaves on the drops point down and end in a single leaf.

8

8 Add darker green to the leaves in the garlands, keeping the shadows consistent with the shading added around the roses.

9

9 Chalk in an oval on each side and on the top of the chest, drawing around an oval plate if you have one that is a suitable size. Paint the leaves on the sides so that they appear to grow from the bottom, up each side and meet at the top.

10 Paint over the whole chest and drawers with antiquing fluid. Do not worry if you do not like the effect because it can be removed with mineral spirits without harming the underlying paint.

11 Use clean, dry paper towel to wipe off the excess antiquing fluid. How much you remove is a matter of choice, but it is a good idea to wipe off more around the main design while leaving the edges slightly dirtier. Leave to dry for 24 hours before sealing with oil-based varnish.

PIANO STOOL

This piano stool was found in a secondhand store, and although it looked very battered, it was such a pretty shape that it was well worth painting. It still had some of its original shellac varnish on it, which was removed with coarse sandpaper before the wood was sealed with acrylic primer/undercoat (see also the Chair, page 22).

You will need
◊ Piano stool
◊ Acrylic primer/undercoat
◊ Latex paint – coral
◊ House-painter's brush
◊ Chalk
◊ Ruler
◊ Tracing paper and pencil
◊ Masking tape
◊ Graphite tracing-down paper
◊ Artists' acrylic paints – white, raw umber and burnt umber
◊ Design brush – No. 4
◊ Coachliner
◊ Colored varnish and varnish brush

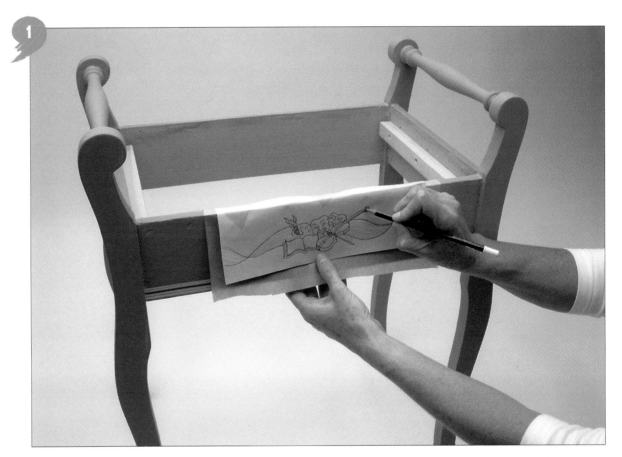

1 Apply a coat of coral latex to the primed piano stool and, when it is dry, use chalk to mark the center of the back and front panels. Copy the design (see page 48) and hold the tracing paper in position with masking tape. Use tracing-down paper to transfer the design.

2 Block in each element of the design separately, bearing in mind that you must have a consistent imaginary light source. Use white paint for the book, and shade the pages where they bend by blending in some raw umber. The artist's palette and brushes are painted in the same way, but they are slightly darker to make them stand out against the book.

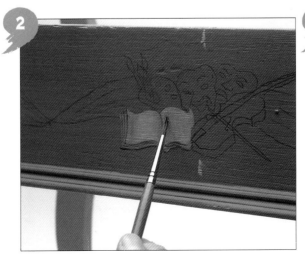

3 Mix burnt umber with a little white to paint the violin. The side of the violin and the details are painted in burnt umber only. The masks are painted white and shaded in the same way as the book, with burnt umber used to pick out the features.

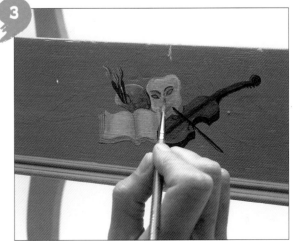

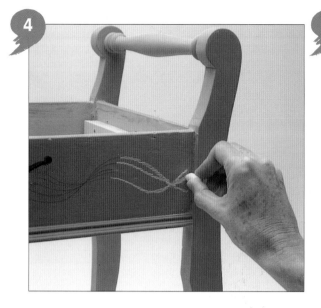

4 If the lines of the staves of music are not long enough for your piano stool, use chalk to draw longer lines. You can easily wipe off chalk lines with which you are not satisfied. Try to balance the design by making the curves in the lines symmetrical.

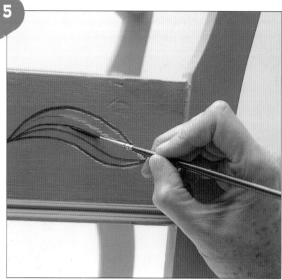

5 Use a coachliner and burnt umber to paint in the lines of the staves.

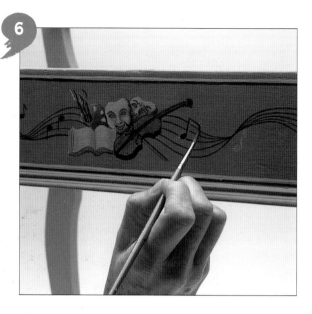

6 Plan the position of the notes in chalk before painting them in with a fine brush.

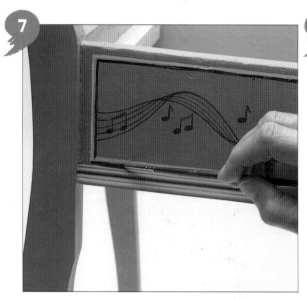

7 Make a border around the whole pattern by painting a thick white line with a coachliner. Use raw umber to draw in lines inside the top and left-hand white lines and outside the bottom and right-hand white lines to give the effect of a molded panel.

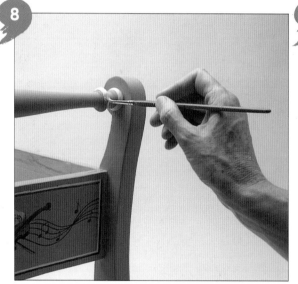

8 Pick out the moldings in white. Take care not to paint right up to the angle where it joins a straight section because it is very difficult to avoid a ragged edge.

9 Use either a colored varnish or make your own, by mixing clear varnish with a little raw umber. If the varnish is oil-based, use artists' oil paint; if the varnish is water-based, use artists' acrylic paint diluted with an appropriate solvent before adding to varnish.

TEMPLATES

This book belongs to